A city adventure in ...
Beijing

by Amy Allatson

Words in **blue** can be found in the glossary on page 24.

Contents

©2017
Book Life
King's Lynn
Norfolk PE30 4LS

ISBN: 978-1-78637-054-9

Written by:
Amy Allatson

Edited by:
Charlie Ogden

Designed by:
Natalie Carr

What is a City?

Cities are **urban settlements**. They are bigger than towns and villages in size and have larger **populations**. Cities are usually very busy places with lots of buildings.

In every country there are cities and most countries have a capital city. Cities are often home to people from many different **cultures**.

WHAT IS A CAPITAL CITY?
A capital city is usually home to a country's government.

8569912

Where is Beijing?

Beijing is the second biggest city in China. It is located in the north of China.

Population:
Over 11.5 Million

Famous landmark:
Forbidden City

Language:
Mandarin

Coldest months:
December to January

Average temperature:
3°C

Warmest months:
June to July

Average temperature:
27°C

Beijing

Hangzhou

Shanghai

Hong Kong

Flight No.

AM A24-11-88-9

Beijing is the capital city of China. Many **tourists** visit Beijing each year for its **history** and culture.

Where and Why?

The city of Beijing began over 3,000 years ago. However, people have lived in the area for over 500,000 years.

Beijing used to be called Peking.

Beijing is home to many ancient landmarks.

Beijing has had many leaders, known as emperors. It is also home to many **ancient landmarks** that the emperors have built over the years.

9

Sightseeing in Beijing

This was called the Forbidden City because only the emperor could allow people to go inside the city walls.

There are many things to see and do in Beijing. Tourists can visit the Forbidden City, which is a city built out of wood.

Tourists can also visit the Great Wall of China. The Great Wall of China is a huge stone wall that is over 5,500 miles long.

The Great Wall of China took over 2,000 years to build.

Food in Beijing

One of the most famous dishes eaten in Beijing is Peking duck. Peking duck is roasted duck breast that is served with a special sauce, called hoisin sauce.

Peking duck is usually eaten with cucumber, spring onion and hoisin sauce.

Chinese food is usually eaten with two wooden sticks, called chopsticks.

Chinese dumplings called jiaozi are eaten all over China. They are usually filled with meat or vegetables and flavoured with **spices**.

Travelling Around Beijing

People travel around Beijing on a *railway network* called the Beijing Subway. The trains travel underneath the city at very high speeds.

← 开往宋家庄
To SONGJIAZHUANG

Rickshaw

Lots of people travel around Beijing on bicycles and rickshaws. Rickshaws are taxis that are pulled along by drivers on bicycles.

Where do People Live in Beijing?

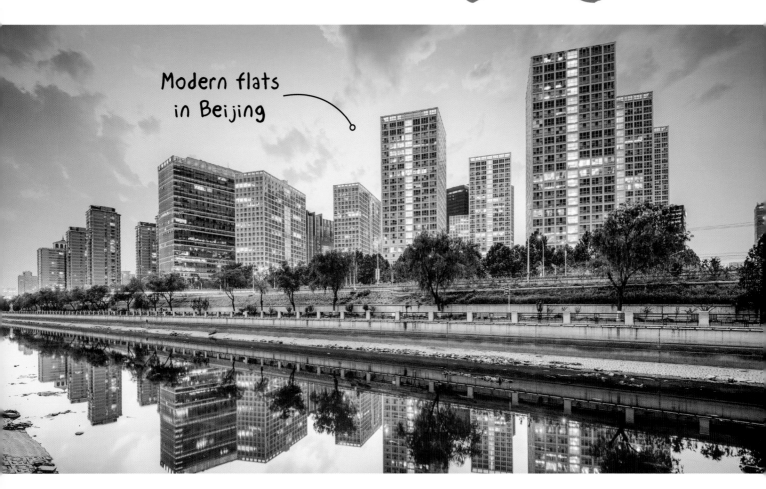

Modern flats in Beijing

Lots of people who live in Beijing live in **modern** flats in very tall buildings.

There are also many traditional houses in Beijing, called courtyard houses. They are usually made up of four houses with a garden or courtyard in the middle.

Traditional buildings are often decorated in bright colours and patterns.

FLIGHT NO:

Geography

Beijing is built between two **mountain ranges**.
The Yongding River flows through the city.

Jingshan Park is one of the highest places in the city.
There are many temples and gardens in the park.

Out and About

Some parts of the Great Wall of China are over 2,000 years old.

There are lots of things to see and do in Beijing. People can visit the Great Wall of China, which has lots of tall towers to view the city from above.

Beihai Park is one of the largest traditional gardens in China. The park also has many temples and a large lake with boats.

What is It?

Can you write down what's in the pictures below?

These are all things that are found in Beijing.

Quick Quiz

1. How many people live in Beijing?

2. How long is the Great Wall of China?

3. How can people travel around the city?

4. What river flows through Beijing?

5. What are Beijing's traditional houses called?

Glossary

ancient landmarks	very old and important buildings
cultures	attitudes and beliefs of a country or a group of people
government	a group of people who make a country's rules and laws
history	events in the past
modern	something from present or recent times
mountain ranges	groups of connected mountains
populations	the number of people who live in certain places
railway network	connected railway tracks and stations
spices	ingredients used to add flavour to food
tourists	people who are away from home because they are on holiday
traditional	something that has continued in a culture for a long time without changing
urban settlements	places where lots of people live and work, like a town or city

Index

Photo Credits